Holyhead-Dun...
From Car Fe...
1965-1996

Miles Cowsill · John Hendy

Published by
Ferry Publications

ISBN 1 87194738 8

Ferry Publications, PO Box 9, Narberth, Pembrokeshire SA68 0YT

Holyhead–Dun Laoghaire – From Car Ferry to HSS

INTRODUCTION

The 57 miles of Irish Sea between Holyhead and Dun Laoghaire are steeped in interest and history. Like most long-established links, it was the coming of the Chester & Holyhead Railway in 1848 that provided direct communication between London and Holyhead and thence the need to provide improved steamship services to Ireland. As with today, competition then existed in the form of the City of Dublin Steam Packet Company who were to remain a thorn in the side of the railway company for seventy years.

Initially the railway company (whose services were taken over by the London & North Western Railway (L.N.W.R.) in 1856) operated a 5 hour passenger, cargo and cattle operation in addition to the twice daily Mail service operated by the Dublin company. The Irish Mail steamers operated from the Admiralty Pier while the railway vessels used a shallow creek adjacent to the outer harbour which was to become Holyhead Inner Harbour.

In October 1860, an improved mail service was introduced by the City of Dublin S.P. Co. and a crossing of 3 hours 45 minutes duration was offered. Now unable to compete, in October the following year the railway service was switched to Dublin (North Wall).

In order to try and secure the important Mail contract, the L.N.W.R. greatly improved both the Inner Harbour and station at Holyhead (which included the construction of a new railway hotel) and followed with similar improvements at North Wall. New ships, two for a new Express Day Service (the *Rose* and the *Shamrock*) and two for an Express Night Service (the *Lily* and the *Violet*) were added from Laird's Birkenhead yard in 1876 and 1880.

Holyhead Station. Passengers embark for the Dublin boat in the early years of this century. (*The Henry Maxwell collection*)

To compete with the City of Dublin co's new *Ulster*, *Leinster* *Munster* and *Connaught*, the L.N.W.R. added the *Cambria* in 1897, followed three years later by the *Hibernia* and *Anglia* with the *Scotia* in 1902. All four came from Denny's Dumbarton yard

High harbour dues at Dublin saw the L.N.W.R. switch its Da Express service back to Kingstown as from April 1908 although the cargo services continued to run to North Wall. In 1920, the rival City of Dublin company finally lost the Irish Mail contract to the L.N.W.R. and four new 25 knot ships appeared from Denny's

Following the creation of the Irish Free State in 1921 Kingstown was renamed Dun Laoghaire and in 1923 the London Midland & Scottish Railway Company (L.M.S.) was created taking over the ships and services operated by the erstwhile London &

Holyhead–Dun Laoghaire – From Car Ferry to HSS

North Western Railway.

The L.M.S. became part of the nationalised British Railways in 1948 and the *Cambria* and *Hibernia* became the last two traditional passenger/mail vessels to be constructed for the route in 1949.

Changing traffic trends were reflected in 1965 with the introduction of the route's first purpose-built vehicle ferry, the *Holyhead Ferry I*. Even then, this was still only a seasonal operation and the vast majority of travellers would continue to arrive and depart by train. The passenger ships offered a popular sleeping on board facility allowing travellers to embark long before the ships sailed in order that they might gain a good night's sleep. Each ship operated a single night time crossing and during daylight remained in port at either Holyhead or Dun Laoghaire.

What could now appear to be outmoded practices finally ceased in 1975 and the coming of the route's own *St. Columba* (later *Stena Hibernia* and then *Stena Adventurer*) totally transformed the historic link finishing a style of service which had barely altered in 100 years.

Sealink was sold to Sea Containers in 1984 and following a further sale to Stena Line in 1990, high speed craft were introduced for the first time.

Initially the *Stena Sea Lynx* took up the route, followed in 1994 by her larger sister the *Stena Sea Lynx II*. Finally the first of the revolutionary HSS 1500 craft, the *Stena Explorer* entered service in 1996 requiring completely new methods of operation and port infrastructure.

This publication traces the demise of the historic passenger-orientated link between Holyhead and Dun Laoghaire and the birth of the car ferry service which after thirty years eventually blossomed to produce the revolutionary HSS. The historic

An impressive view of the **Stena Explorer** at her berth at Holyhead. Passengers disembark and embark through covered walkways direct onto the vessel at both the Welsh and Irish ports. *(Stena Line)*

crossing has undergone a transport revolution and both ports have been modified to meet the exciting new challenge which Stena's 21st century craft presents to them.

Miles Cowsill,
Narberth,
Pembrokeshire.

John Hendy,
Staplehurst,
Kent.

December 1996

Seen from the Station Hotel, the **Cambria**, **Princess Maud** and **Slieve League** at Holyhead
(Malcolm McRonald collection)

Holyhead–Dun Laoghaire – From Car Ferry to HSS

SETTING THE SCENE

Prior to 1842 the main sea route to Dublin from England was via Liverpool. A House of Commons Select Committee looked into the service offered between Britain and Ireland in that year and recommended that a more rapid service should be offered. The Committee were happy with the existing service, but felt that once the railway had been opened through to North Wales, an alternative service should be considered to cut down the time at sea, thus making way for a quicker link between the two capital cities.

Among several of the schemes considered was the construction of a railway line from Chester, along the North Wales coast, to the island of Anglesey and on to Holyhead on Holy Island. A year later, after the Select Committee's findings had been published, the plan became a reality, once the problem of crossing the Menai Strait had been solved by the noted Victorian engineer Robert Stephenson.

The new line to Holyhead was opened in 1848 and a subsidiary company of the Chester and Holyhead Railway was formed to provide a link to Ireland. Four paddle steamers were commissioned for this service - the *Hibernia, Scotia, Anglia* and the *Cambria*. By August 1848 the Admiralty Packets had been transferred from Liverpool to the newly established route. The service from Holyhead was established to Kingstown, which was renamed Dun Laoghaire during the 1920's.

By the end of the 19th Century the London North Western Railway was operating a service with four new ships which had

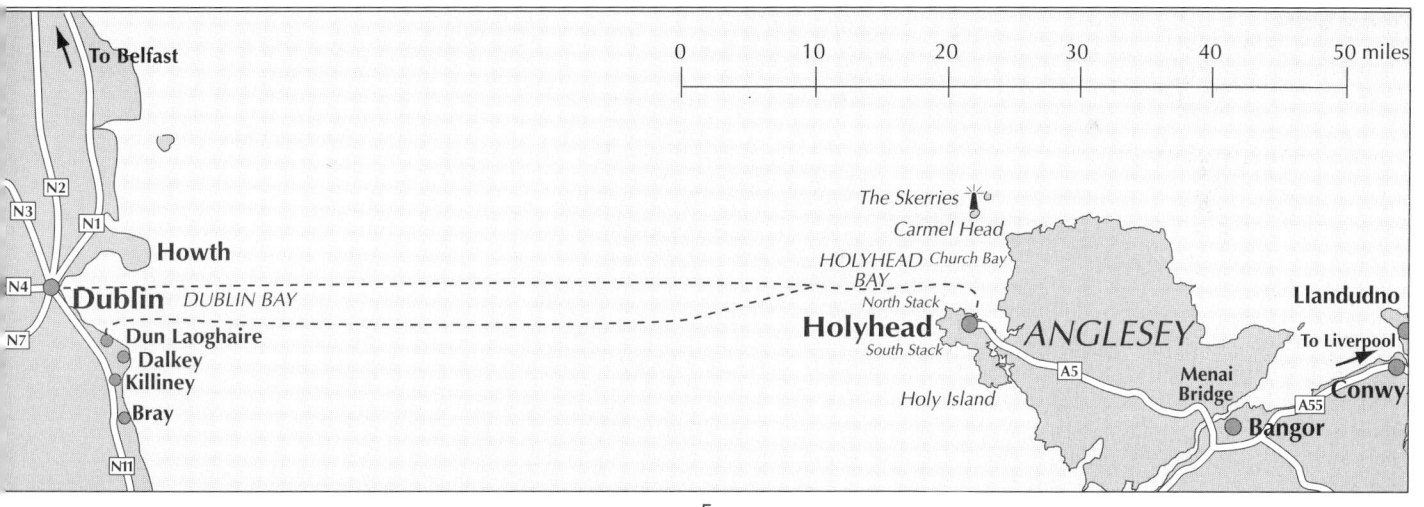

Holyhead–Dun Laoghaire – From Car Ferry to HSS

been built in the light of fierce competition from the rival Company who operated out of Holyhead, the City of Dublin Company. The new quartet of Denny-built ships were to maintain the service until the First World War.

Within a few days of the outbreak of the First World War the four ships *Cambria*, *Hibernia*, *Anglia* and *Scotia* were requisitioned by the Admiralty. The City of Dublin Company would have had the monopoly of the Dublin service during the War, had the LNWR not transferred three passenger/cargo ships *Rathmore*, *Greenore* and *Galtee More*.

The *Hibernia* and the *Anglia* were lost during the Great War, but the *Cambria* and *Scotia* were returned to the Railway company in 1918.

Following the war the L.N.W.R. went back to Wm. Denny and Brothers for four new ships. The two pre-war "Kingdom Class" vessels were renamed, so that the traditional names for the route could be maintained. The first of the new ships *Anglia* was delivered at 3,460 tons gross (nearly twice the size of the older ships) in 1920, followed by the *Hibernia*, *Cambria* and *Scotia*. The new vessels had a service speed of 25 knots and were amongst the most beautiful of all cross Channel steamers ever built. The new ships were to finally obtain the mail contract for the L.N.W.R. Meanwhile the City of Dublin Company ceased trading in 1920, after heavy war losses of their fleet during the First World War.

In 1923 the service was taken over by London Midland and Scottish Railway Company under the amalgamations and re-organisations of the British railways during the early twenties. The new company took a good look at operations at Holyhead and its four ships on the passenger and mail runs to Ireland. It was decided for reasons, most probably of economy, that only three ships were required on the route and the *Anglia* was withdrawn.

Above: A magnificent view of the London and North Western Railway Company's **Hibernia** (II) arriving off the Irish coast. *(The Henry Maxwell collection)*
Below: The **Princess Maud** pictured at Holyhead in the early fifties. *(Ferry Publications Library)*

Holyhead–Dun Laoghaire – From Car Ferry to HSS

Above: The classic passenger vessel **Hibernia** berthed at the departure berth in the inner harbour at Holyhead. This view shows the hotel built in 1880 at the end of the harbour adjacent to the railway station. *(Jim Ashby collection)*

The Smoking room on board the **Hibernia**. *(Jim Ashby collection)*

First-class tea lounge on board the **Hibernia**. *(Jim Ashby collection)*

Holyhead–Dun Laoghaire – From Car Ferry to HSS

*A wonderful view of the port of Holyhead and its fleet in the late sixties. This picture shows from the left the **Harrogate**, **Slieve Donard**, **Cambria**, **Hibernia**, **Slieve Bloom**, **Slieve More** and **Holyhead Ferry I**. (Jim Ashby collection)*

Sadly she was only to see service during peak periods after the re-organisation of the route and in 1924 she was laid up at Barrow for ten years before being broken up. After 1924 the *Duke of Abercorn* was transferred from Heysham to cover during holiday periods.

In 1932 the three remaining "Kingdom Class" ships received modernisation of their passenger areas. The three sisters continued the mail-passenger services until the outbreak of the Second World War. During the war the Holyhead route was maintained as far as possible by the *Hibernia*, while the *Cambria* was transferred to Heysham to cover the Belfast service. The *Scotia* was lost during the evacuation at Dunkerque.

In 1946 the L.M.S. placed a long overdue order with Harland and Wolff for two 4,900 ton motor ships. Meanwhile, the *Princess Maud* (in place of the *Scotia*) was transferred from Stranraer to Holyhead to assist the older ships before the new tonnage arrived.

The new *Hibernia* was launched first on 22nd July 1948

Holyhead–Dun Laoghaire – From Car Ferry to HSS

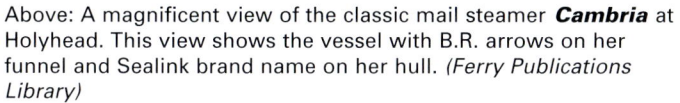

Above: A magnificent view of the classic mail steamer **Cambria** at Holyhead. This view shows the vessel with B.R. arrows on her funnel and Sealink brand name on her hull. *(Ferry Publications Library)*

Top Right: The **Hibernia** laid up at Heysham at the end of her career with Sealink. *(Malcolm McRonald)*

Right: The **Cambria** leaving Dun Laoghaire for Holyhead on 10th June 1967. *(Malcolm McRonald)*

Holyhead–Dun Laoghaire – From Car Ferry to HSS

entering service on 14th April 1949, initially with the *Hibernia II* until she was replaced by the new *Cambria* in May the same year. Both vessels were designed to carry some 2,360 passengers in two classes, with sleeping accommodation consisting of two-berth cabins-de-luxe, one and two-berth cabins for the first-class passengers and two, four and six-berth cabins and open berths for the second-class passengers. Both could maintain a speed of 21 knots and when built they had the distinction of being the largest of the British cross channel ships. They both had a tendency to roll and were both fitted with stabilisers in 1954. The *Princess Maud* remained at Holyhead following the entry into service of the new vessels as the standby ship, but each autumn she returned to Stranraer while the Larne ships went for their refits.

Meanwhile, the old *Hibernia* was withdrawn at the end of 1948 followed by the *Cambria* the following spring. The new post-war ships settled down into an all year round routine with one nightly sailing in each direction with a daylight sailing during the summer, with the *Princess Maud* offering a third sailing during the peak weeks of the summer.

During the winter of 1964/65 the *Hibernia* and *Cambria* underwent a modernisation programme which included renewal of their passenger accommodation, and also the removal of cabins on C Deck, which were replaced with a new second class lounge. On D Deck a new second class Smoke Room and Cafeteria were introduced and on B Deck the former Smoke Rooms of both classes became a Tea Room. The gross tonnage of both ships was increased to 5,284, and following their major refits could accommodate 425 in the first class and 1,830 second class passengers. The ships returned to Holyhead in the new BR livery of red funnels and blue hulls.

Above: The **Princess Maud** and **Hibernia** berthed at the Carlisle Pier, Dun Laoghaire. *(Ferry Publications Library)*

Below: An aerial view showing the newly-opened St. Michael's Pier Terminal at Dun Laoghaire. At the Carlisle Pier the **Holyhead Ferry I** can be seen while to the far right of the picture the original car ferry berth can be seen on the East Pier. *(Jim Ashby collection)*

Holyhead–Dun Laoghaire – From Car Ferry to HSS

CAR FERRY ERA

To meet the growing demand for passengers to take their cars with them during the early sixties, British Rail decided to order the first vehicle-carrying ship in 1964, with drive on/drive off facilities for the Holyhead-Dun Laoghaire route. Hawthorn-Leslie (Shipbuilders) Limited were appointed to build the new ship, which would be able to carry 1,000 passengers and 160 cars. Meanwhile work was to be put in hand for a new berth at Holyhead with a ramp for stern loading at the site of the inner harbour side of the Old Admiralty Pier at Salt Island. Similar arrangements were put in hand at Dun Laoghaire.

The new ship for the car ferry service, the *Holyhead Ferry I* was launched on 17th February 1965. She was late entering service and the newly converted car ferry *Normannia* from Dover opened the new Holyhead-Dun Laoghaire service from 9th to 19th July 1965 until the *Holyhead Ferry I* was able to make her maiden voyage. The vessel offered accommodation for 1,000 one-class passengers, including 2 cabins-de-luxe, 12 one-berth, 15 two-berth and 6 three-berth cabins. Her other facilities included smokeroom/bar forward on the shelter deck, self-service cafeteria on the upper deck, tea-bar/lounge on shelter deck amidships, and a lounge aft on shelter deck. She operated only as a one-class ship, as opposed to the two passenger ships which operated both first and second class travel.

With a gross tonnage of 3,879 and two sets of oil-fired turbines she was able to achieve 19.5 knots. Access to the main car deck was through her stern door. By today's standards, she was a small car ferry with only a capacity for 160 cars. The

*The delay of the **Holyhead Ferry I** meant that the **Normannia** had to open the new car ferry service. She is seen here arriving at the Anglesey port on the inaugural trip of the new service, with the **Princess Maud** astern. (Jim Ashby collection)*

Holyhead–Dun Laoghaire – From Car Ferry to HSS

Holyhead Ferry I soon settled down into her new role and proved a very popular addition. The *Princess Maud* which had been the "third" ship at the port until the arrival of the car ferry, was subsequently withdrawn in September and sold for service in Greek waters. She left Holyhead on 17th September renamed *Venus*.

The main timings of the new car ferry service were 10.45 and 20.15 (Fridays to Saturdays only) from Holyhead during the peak season. This was gradually scaled down until only Friday and Saturday sailings at 10.45 were offered during the first two weeks of October, after which the service was suspended until the next season. British Rail decided that the car ferry service should only be seasonal, until there was sufficient all-year round trade. Once the *Holyhead Ferry I* completed her first season, she was transferred to Stranraer during the early part of 1966 to cover during the refits of the Scottish ships.

The *Holyhead Ferry I* started 1966 at Holyhead on 20th May running on a daily basis to Dun Laoghaire, with extra sailings being operated during the peak weekends of the summer. Meanwhile the passenger ships *Hibernia* and *Cambria* maintained the passenger only and mail services to Ireland. During the winter period while the car ferry service was not running, cars had to be crane-loaded onto the passenger ships. Once again in 1967 the *Holyhead Ferry I* went north to Stranraer.

NEW GROUND

The passenger ship *Hibernia* was briefly transferred to Heysham after Christmas in 1967 to cover for the *Duke of Argyll's* dry docking. This was the first time that the *Hibernia* had left Holyhead in her career, but she was to leave again the next year

A cold Winter scene on the Tyne. This view shows the **Holyhead Ferry I** on the stocks prior to her launch on 17th February 1965. *(Jim Ashby collection)*

12

The **Holyhead Ferry I** on trials prior to entering service. (*Jim Ashby collection*)

Holyhead–Dun Laoghaire – From Car Ferry to HSS

when she was required on the Harwich-Hook of Holland service in October while the *St. George* went for overhaul. Meanwhile, during the winter of 1968/69 the *Holyhead Ferry I* took the place of one of the mail ships running on Mondays, Wednesdays and Fridays from Holyhead.

The car ferry service continued to expand and for the peak season of 1969 it was decided to have two ferries operating the route. The *Dover* was earmarked from the Dover Strait to run with her near sister *Holyhead Ferry I*. However, due to the late arrival of the *Vortigern*, the *Caledonian Princess* had to stand in until the *Dover* could be released.

The *Holyhead Ferry I* and *Dover* were engaged again in a two ship seasonal car ferry working between 22nd May and 19th September. The mainstays of the route were still operated by the overnight passenger only vessels *Cambria* and *Hibernia*.

On 23rd May 1971, fire seriously damaged the 120 year old Britannia Tubular Bridge across the Menai Strait thereby isolating the port of Holyhead from all rail connections. The car ferry service continued but the passenger vessels, along with the rail connected cargo boat operations, were switched to Heysham from where the Dun Laoghaire service operated until the bridge was eventually repaired. A third passenger vessel was required at weekends and this role was filled by the Fishguard steamer *St. David*. B.R. chartered Fisher's *Kingsnorth Fisher* to operate three sailings from Holyhead to Barrow during mid-June to retrieve their eleven trapped locomotives from the Anglesey port.

The Britannia Railway Bridge across the Menai Strait was reopened on 30th January 1972. The traditional mail boat service was then transferred from Heysham and with the *Hibernia* on overhaul at the time, it was left to the *Cambria* (20.45 from Dun Laoghaire) and the *Holyhead Ferry I* to recommence operations at

Above: The **Holyhead Ferry I** - lounge/tea bar. *(Jim Ashby collection)*
Below: The **Holyhead Ferry I** - main bar. *(Jim Ashby collection)*

Holyhead–Dun Laoghaire – From Car Ferry to HSS

Holyhead. The 'HF I' sailed 'light' to Holyhead from Heysham to take up the 03.15 on 31st January.

With the *Duke of Rothesay* not required at Fishguard for the summer, she became the second car ferry at Holyhead. She was to spend a second season at the port the following year opening the seasonal Dun Laoghaire car ferry service on 17th April between the overnight 'mail' runs.

In 1974 British Rail announced that a new £650,000 linkspan would be built in the inner harbour close to the main line railway station at Holyhead thereby allowing both rail and vehicle traffic to use the same vessel at off-peak periods.

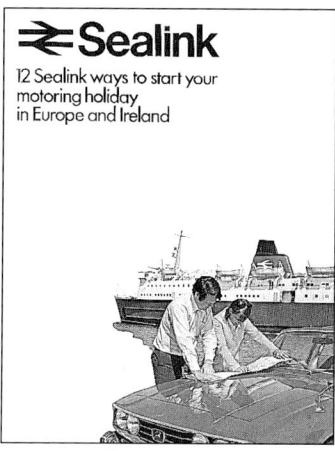

Left: The **Holyhead Ferry I** coming astern at her home port during her first season in service. *(Jim Ashby collection)*

Below: The **Holyhead Ferry I** pictured at the new Salt Island berth in 1965. *(Jim Ashby collection)*

St. Columba (Miles Cowsill)

Holyhead–Dun Laoghaire – From Car Ferry to HSS

THE LARGEST EVER

In late March 1975, British Rail Sealink placed an order with Aalborg Vaerft A/S of Aalborg, Denmark for a new passenger car ferry to be specially designed for service between the ports.

Following the arrival of the *Avalon* at Fishguard in mid-July 1975, the *Duke of Lancaster* switched to Holyhead where she operated the summer service with the *Dover*. Meanwhile the passenger ship *Cambria* was withdrawn from service on 7th September, following the 20.45 from Dun Laoghaire and after which the time-honoured sleeping on-board facilities were withdrawn, other than when the ship was at sea on a scheduled crossing. She arrived at Barrow for lay-up on 31st October. The *Cambria* was sold to the Orri Navigation Company of Saudi Arabia for £350,000 and renamed *Altaif*. After being laid up at Barrow, she arrived in the Mersey on 17th January 1976 to take on bunkers at Tranmere. She foundered in Suez Roads in January 1981. Meanwhile the *Hibernia* completed her season on 5th October. The following day, the traditional 'mailboat' sailings (03.15 from Holyhead and 20.45 from Dun Laoghaire) were taken over by a car ferry on a single vessel working.

On 30th November, the Dublin livestock and general cargo service duly closed, after which the *Isle of Ely* sailed to Barrow for lay-up.

In 1976 the former Holyhead based vessel, the *Holyhead Ferry I* was sent to Swan Hunter's for conversion to a drive-through ship to meet the ever increasing demand on the Dover Strait's operations. On completion of this work, she emerged as the *Earl Leofric*, with increased capacity to 205 cars but with a reduced passenger accommodation of 725.

Arriving in thick fog early on 18th March 1976, the *Avalon*

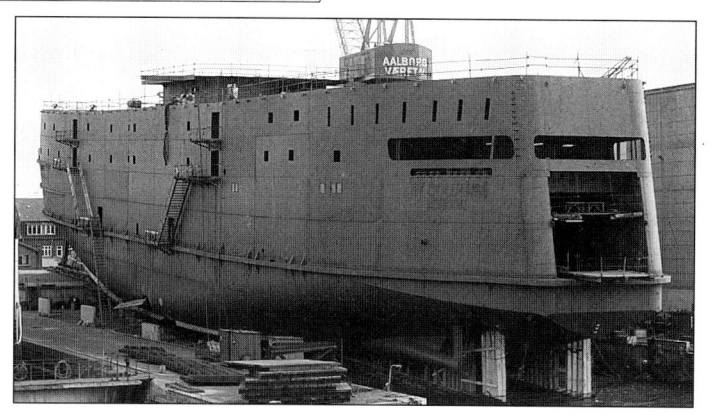

Above: The **St. Columba** seen prior to her launch at Aalborg Vaerft, Denmark on 16th July 1996. *(Jim Ashby collection)*
Below: The **St. Columba** pictured at Holyhead shortly after her arrival from Denmark. This view also shows the former Thoresen vessel **Viking II / Earl William** under conversion at the port for Sealink's Channel Island services. *(Miles Cowsill)*

Holyhead–Dun Laoghaire – From Car Ferry to HSS

Cars discharged from the ***St. Columba*** during her first season in operation. *(Jim Ashby collection)*

which was covering on the route, extensively damaged her bow and had to go off service for two weeks. Her deep draught made berthing in the inner harbour difficult during periods of low water when she was frequently required to sail up to an hour early. The *Dover* was switched from Fishguard to deputise while the spare *Maid of Kent* moved to the St. George's Channel route.

At 00.15 on 3rd October 1976, the *Hibernia* completed her final sailing on the 20.45 from Dun Laoghaire. She was sold to Greek owners, Agapitos Bros., and was renamed *Express Apollon*. She sailed from Holyhead, to the Mersey, to take on bunkers on 1st December. The vessel was broken up at Mumbai, India in 1981.

After a delay of 24 hours, the new vehicle ferry *St. Columba*, named after a 6th century monk and abbot who established monasteries in Ireland and Scotland, was launched by Mrs Joan Kirby, wife of the then Managing Director of Sealink at Aalborg on 17th July 1976. She arrived at Holyhead next year from the builders on 6th April.

The inaugural sailing of the *St. Columba*, Sealink's largest ever ship in the fleet, took place on 27th April 1977 with a party of special guests. She departed from Holyhead at 14.00 for Dun Laoghaire under the command of Captain Leonard R. Evans, and arrived at Dun Laoghaire at 17.30. The blessing of the *St. Columba* by parish priests of Dun Laoghaire took place the next day.

British Rail's Chairman, Mr Peter Parker, was aboard the *St. Columba* on the inaugural sailing and on arrival at Dun Laoghaire welcomed aboard the Prime Minister of the Republic of Ireland, Mr Liam Cosgrave.

The £19 million *St. Columba* was built as a two-class multi-purpose ship and offered a higher standard of comfort and

The **St. Columba** arrives at Holyhead from Dun Laoghaire. This view shows the stern bridge which was built to allow her Master to take the ship out astern at the Anglesey port. *(Jim Ashby collection)*

Holyhead–Dun Laoghaire – From Car Ferry to HSS

facilities than ever before on Sealink's Irish Sea routes.

Mr David Kirby, British Rail Shipping & International Services Division's General Manager, speaking to the press on her maiden voyage, said, "Our faith in an increasing passenger and car ferry traffic to and from Ireland, together with growing Ro-Ro commercial vehicle traffic, is exemplified by the new *St Columba* and justifies our long-term investment plans to provide more capacity on the Irish Sea. *St. Columba*, the pride of Sealink's fleet on the Irish Sea, gives us the additional capacity we need to realise the full potential of the route."

Her original capacity was for 1,600 passengers - augmented to 2,400 in the peak season - with comfortable under-cover seats for all passengers. The vehicle was designed with bow and stern access and her car deck could take 335 cars or 36 x 40 ft. road haulage vehicles or a mixture of the two.

She offered an impressive range of passenger amenities, including well-appointed lounges and two bars, which were named Lansdowne and Cardiff Arms on the inaugural voyage. A waiter-service restaurant was provided in her original layout and there were four buffet lounges equipped with self-service rotating "carousels" serving hot and cold meals - a new feature on Sealink ships enabling much faster service of meals to passengers, it was claimed at the time. A nursing mothers' room, shopping areas, three television lounges and a discotheque were also part of passenger areas.

Little more than a year after entering service for Sealink between Holyhead and Dun Laoghaire, the *St. Columba* carried her millionth passenger. The new vessel was also to attract more holidaymakers wanting to take their cars to Ireland. The boom in traffic across the Irish Sea showed healthy increases in passengers and vehicles on the Holyhead-Dun Laoghaire route

Above: The **St. Columba** - discotheque. *(Jim Ashby collection)*
Below: The **St. Columba** - second-class Pullman lounge. *(Jim Ashby collection)*

Holyhead–Dun Laoghaire – From Car Ferry to HSS

The **Duke of Rothesay** seen here leaving Holyhead following her conversion to a car ferry. *(Ferry Publications Library)*

over the next couple of years. Meanwhile, Sealink chartered the freighter *Transbaltica* to relieve the *St. Columba* of some of her lorry traffic. During the autumn, the *Dalriada* arrived in place of the *Transbaltica* to support the *St. Columba*.

The *Duke of Lancaster* took over the Holyhead–Dun Laoghaire service at the beginning of October when Sealink were forced to withdraw the *St. Columba* because of propeller shaft problems. The 'Duke' was employed to handle passengers and cars while the *Dalriada* supported her in a freight mode. During the Irish public holiday weekend at the end of October, the *Maid of Kent* was brought into service to provide additional capacity. The *St. Columba* eventually returned to service on 8th November 1978.

During March 1979, the chartered *Stena Timer* (a near sister of the *Darnia* at Stranraer) was brought into service at Holyhead to support the *Avalon* with freight sailings. She had previously operated as P&O's *Jaguar* on their Fleetwood–Larne service. A second visit was made by the ship from 21st May until 25th September as a back-up to the *St. Columba* and she remained on the service.

Meanwhile the *Lord Warden* returned to the Holyhead/Fishguard–Dun Laoghaire service but not on the Rosslare route as in the previous season. She completed her service with a sailing from Dun Laoghaire to Holyhead on 8th September before sailing to Newhaven two days later.

The *St. Columba* broke down with gear-box troubles on 30th October, passengers and cars had to be diverted to the Fishguard and Liverpool routes. The *Maid of Kent* was introduced the following day and had to be assisted by the *Stena Timer* before the 'Columba' resumed within the week.

The chartered ro–ro vessel *Stena Timer* left Holyhead for Stranraer on 7th February 1980 after assisting the *Avalon* to cover

Holyhead–Dun Laoghaire – From Car Ferry to HSS

The **Avalon** seen arriving at Holyhead during her last season with Sealink. *(Ferry Publications Library)*

The **Holyhead Ferry I's** near sister the **Dover** was employed on several occasions on the Holyhead-Dun Laoghaire route during the sixties and seventies. *(Nick Robins)*

for the *St. Columba* which was late back from her Clydeside overhaul.

The Holyhead–Dun Laoghaire route was seriously disrupted after the *St. Columba* suffered a further serious engine failure at the Irish port on 21st May with all sailings cancelled until the *Avalon* could be brought into service the following day. The *Avalon* then experienced boiler troubles and had to be withdrawn from operations. Cargo was shifted by using the *Lagan Bridge* (from Heysham) and the Harwich train ferry *Cambridge Ferry* which was in the port undergoing overhaul at the time. The *Ailsa Princess* was sent from Stranraer to take up the service as from 31st May, her first ever spell away from the route for which she was built. Three days later the *Avalon* was repaired and she was able to resume services in the absence of the *St. Columba* which

was off service for three weeks. She eventually returned to service on 12th June.

On 25th September, the new £16 million *St. David*, the last of the quartet of ferries ordered at Harland & Wolff, was duly launched at Belfast. Already some four months behind schedule, it was still uncertain whether or not the vessel would be employed on the Fishguard–Rosslare service as originally planned. The *St. David* was named by Mrs. Ruth Fowler, wife of British Railways Board member Mr. Derek Fowler. The three other ships of the series were also at Belfast at the time of the launch. The short sea sisters the *St. Anselm* and *St. Christopher* were fitting-out while the slightly smaller *Galloway Princess* was receiving shaft and propeller attention in dry dock.

After completing Holyhead-Dun Laoghaire relief sailings on

Holyhead–Dun Laoghaire – From Car Ferry to HSS

8th September, the *Avalon* was sent for lay-up at Barrow on 24th September with an uncertain future. The ship was later sold for scrap at Gadani Beach in Pakistan and left as the *Valon* in December.

Sealink's third new ferry from Harland & Wolff, the *St. Christopher*, was due to make her maiden voyage between Dover and Calais in March 1981. Due to problems with refit schedules on the Irish Sea and with the *St. Columba* breaking down again, the new Dover vessel sailed directly from her builders to Rosslare for berthing trials and then to Holyhead to cover the absence of the *St. Columba*, before making her maiden commercial voyage on 17th March. On the return of the Danish-built ship, the *St. Christopher* relieved the *Stena Normandica* at Fishguard on 19th March. The *St. Christopher* was to prove an excellent vessel whilst at the Pembrokeshire port, especially during some very inclement weather at the start of April. On the return of the *Stena Normandica*, she then sailed south to join her sister the *St. Anselm* on the Dover-Calais 'Flagship Service'.

Meanwhile, the *Earl Siward*, which had been sharing the Newhaven lay-up berth with her sister the *Earl Leofric* (ex *Holyhead Ferry I*), was sent to Holyhead for dry docking before supporting the *St. Columba* with relief sailings as from 22nd June. This was necessary following further delays in the construction of the *St. David*, which was now earmarked as a Holyhead vessel.

The *Earl Siward* was eventually replaced on 9th July by the chartered Swedish ferry *Prinsessan Desiree* which remained on station until the entry into service of the new ship from Belfast at 09.00 on 10th August.

Above: The **Lagan Bridge** at Holyhead in June 1980. Her sister the **Lune Bridge** was on the run later in the year. *(Dick Richards)*
Below: In March 1991 the **St. Christopher** made her maiden voyage on the Holyhead-Dun Laoghaire route due to technical problems with the **St. Columba**. *(Dick Richards)*

Overleaf: The launch of the **St. David** at Harland & Wolff on 25th September 1980. *(Ferry Publications Library)*

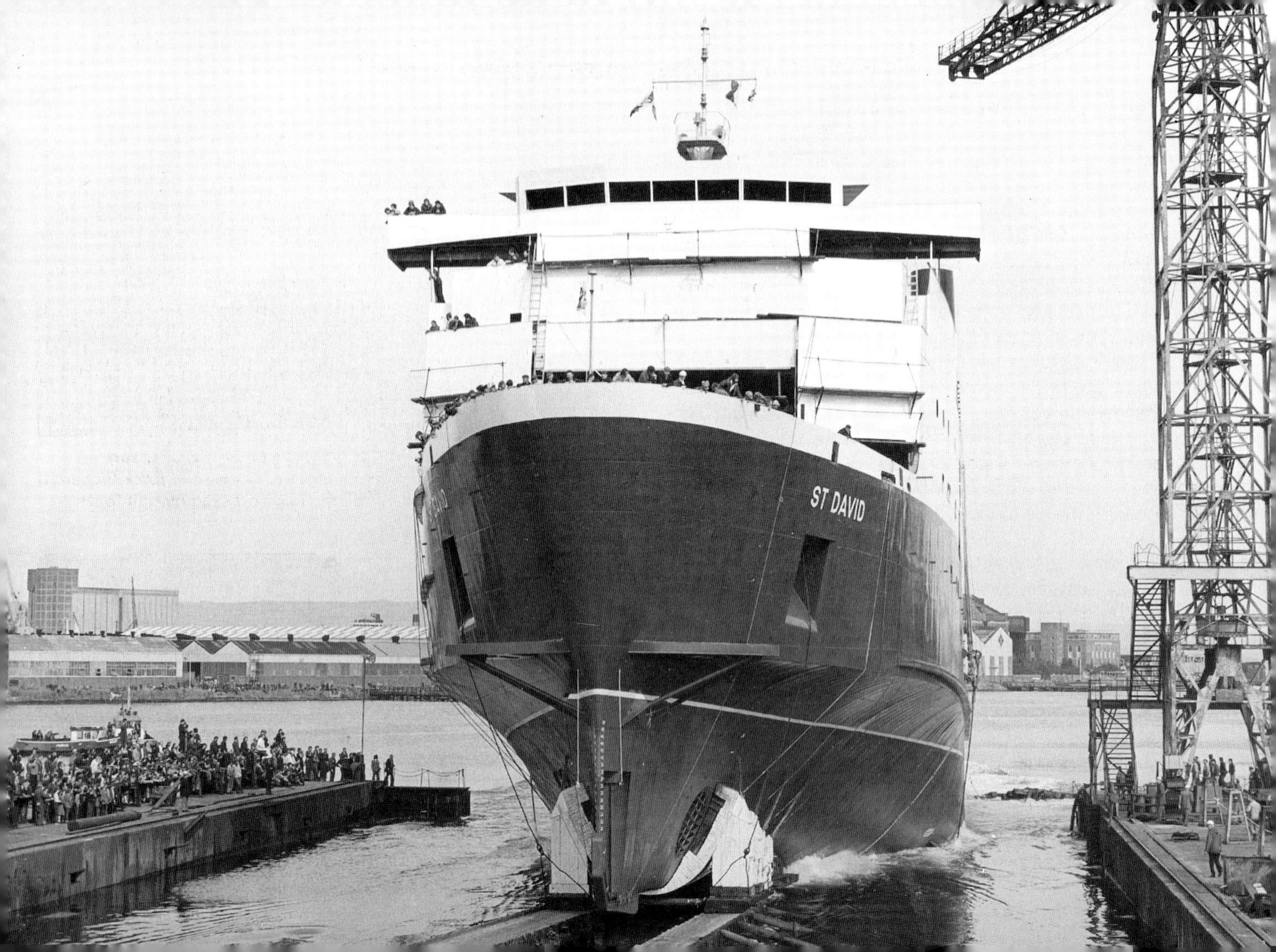
ST DAVID

Holyhead–Dun Laoghaire – From Car Ferry to HSS

ENTER THE SAINT FOR HOLYHEAD

Sealink's *St. David*, the last of the £64 million quartet of vessels built at Harland & Wolff, displaced the *St. Columba* from the Holyhead–Dun Laoghaire winter service. Within a very short period of time, it became clear that the new vessel would be a more economic unit for the winter schedules and the *St. Columba* was laid up.

The *St. David* differed from her near sisters at Dover as her restaurant was forward in an area occupied by the main bar in the Dover Strait vessels. At the time of the ship entering service, she also boasted a 55 seat cinema and a duty-free supermarket, which neither Dover vessel claimed. Like her half-sisters, the vessel also included specially designed internal ramps to give easier access to the upper vehicle deck as neither Holyhead nor Dun Laoghaire had double-deck linkspans. She was also fitted with a stern bridge for docking at the Anglesey port.

With continued losses from B&I Line on their Irish services, the company looked for better utilisation of their tonnage on the central corridor. Sealink were approached to start a new ferry service from Dublin to Holyhead using the Dublin vessels *Leinster* and *Connacht*. The planned new service would allow the Dublin ship to sail by daylight to Anglesey and return before sailing overnight on the established Dublin-Liverpool service. This would allow the company better utilisation of their vessels. The announcement of the service was greeted with hostility by Sealink staff at Holyhead. The first sailings of B&I to Holyhead were to be delayed with a series of opposition tactics at the Anglesey port. The *Connacht* tried to enter Holyhead for berthing trials on 5th March 1982 but failed and also failed again when trying an initial crossing with passengers and vehicles some two

Above: Prior to the arrival of the **St. David**, the **Princessan Desiree** was chartered to support the **St. Columba**. *(Dick Richards)*
Below: The **St. David** arrives at Holyhead dressed overall for the first time. *(Dick Richards)*

The **St. David** seen on trials in the Irish Sea. *(Ferry Publications Library)*

Holyhead–Dun Laoghaire – From Car Ferry to HSS

days later, when Sealink staff blocked the harbour entrance with a group of small boats. The *Leinster* fared no better on 9th March before the B&I crews took retaliatory action at Dun Laoghaire. The *St. David* upon arriving at Dun Laoghaire on 8th March found her way blocked by the B&I vessel *Munster*, which had sailed light with a full crew from Dublin without management permission. The *St. David* was forced to return to Holyhead and tried again next morning to dock, only to find the *Munster* in position again. Finally, the crew of the *Munster* allowed the *St. David* into the port as there was a sick passenger on board. Sealink then announced a suspension of services pending further talks with B&I and also agreed to attempt no more Holyhead sailings until matters were resolved. Continued opposition at Holyhead to the new B&I service saw Sealink dismissing 38 dockers. The opposition to the new service also came at the same time as Sealink announced plans to close the repair facilities at the port.

Meanwhile, the Holyhead vessel *St. Columba* was due to be sent to Pembrokeshire for the refit of the *Stena Normandica*, this was to be her first and only visit away from her home port. Crews of the vessel feared that the ship might not return to North Wales as the *St. David* was proving a very effective ship on the route and with the new service planned by B&I there might not be a need for the vessel there any longer. Management were forced to give assurances to the crews of the Danish-built ship that she would be retained during the summer period at Holyhead, before she was allowed to leave the port to cover for the overhaul of the Fishguard ship.

Following extensive talks between management and unions on both sides of the Irish Sea, B&I were finally able to start their new daylight service from Dublin to Holyhead on 6th April. The

Above: The **Ailsa Princess** at the Salt Island berth on 23rd October 1982. *(Dick Richards)*

Below: The **St. David** seen here bow in at the Salt Island berth at Holyhead. *(Dick Richards)*

Holyhead–Dun Laoghaire – From Car Ferry to HSS

Connacht arrived for berthing trials on 5th April and the first commercial crossing was covered by the *Leinster* the following day. While services were suspended in March on the Holyhead–Dun Laoghaire service, the *St. David* was sent for a refit and alterations to her passenger accommodation to increase her capacity. Following her stint at Fishguard, the *St. Columba* reopened the Holyhead–Dun Laoghaire service after an agreement had been reached between Sealink and B&I.

Despite the fears of those at Holyhead that the new B&I service would see traffic being taken from the established service of Sealink, the two ship operation using the *St. David* as a one-class vessel and the *St. Columba* as a first and second class ship was extended due to increased trade on the link.

On 21st October the *Ailsa Princess* arrived at Holyhead to release the *St. Columba* for conversion into a one class ship. The extensive internal changes were carried out at her home port, which included the creation of a new Pullman lounge, lorry drivers' lounge and restaurant, improvements to the self-service restaurant and an enlargement of the duty-free areas. The ending of the two-class service brought the route in line with the other operations on the Irish Sea.

During early 1983 the *St. David* was sent to Stranraer to deputise for the refits of the vessels at the port. She then went to Fishguard to cover for the refit of the *Stena Normandica* before sailing to Dover to cover the conversion period of her near sister, *St. Christopher*. This allowed the *St. Columba* to take up her key role again as the flagship at Holyhead.

The spare French ferry *Villandry* deputised for the *St. Columba* on 12th/13th August after the larger ship had gone off service with problems to her starboard engine.

The SNCF ferry **Villandry** seen at the Carlisle Pier, Dun Laoghaire on 12th August 1983. *(Philip Booth)*

The **St. Columba** leaving Dun Laoghaire for Wales. *(John Hendy)*

Holyhead–Dun Laoghaire – From Car Ferry to HSS

PRIVATISATION

In readiness for privatisation, on their reappearance from overhaul, units of the Sealink U.K. Ltd. fleet all appeared without the B.R. double arrow logo on their funnels. Four ships initially appeared with the all-white livery and blue funnels: the *St. Nicholas*, *Hengist*, *Horsa* and *Stena Normandica*.

Front runners for purchase of Sealink U.K. Ltd. were a consortium headed by the National Freight Corporation, James Fisher & Sons Ltd. and senior Sealink management but July 1984 saw Sealink U.K. Ltd. sold to Sea Containers of Bermuda for just £66 million. The sale included 37 ships, 10 harbours, including Holyhead, and 24 routes. In future the company would trade as Sealink British Ferries and a subsidiary company British Ferries Ltd. was set-up. A general reappraisal was duly made of all routes and the ships which operated them.

In a letter to all Sealink staff, James Sherwood outlined his plans for the company. On the Irish Sea, the Fishguard–Rosslare route would be expanded and larger Holyhead ferries were needed. The unprofitable lo–lo services from Holyhead to Belfast and Dublin would be revived by larger Sea Containers ships and Stranraer would see the replacement of the *Antrim Princess*. After years of under-investment, it appeared that Sealink was about to be revitalised.

During early February 1985 Sealink British Ferries and B&I Line announced that they had concluded discussions aimed at solving over-capacity on the Irish Sea. Talks had started during December against a background of achieving sailings for both rival companies on bringing frequency of service more in line with demand.

Certain reductions on the daylight sailings were made at Fishguard, whilst B&I Line's Rosslare–Pembroke Dock service was suspended during the company's overhaul programme and traffic was transferred to Fishguard under the agreement. Meanwhile, on 15th April, Sealink British Ferries acquired the *Stena Normandica* from Stena Line and shortly afterwards she was renamed *St. Brendan*.

In a further move the following year, Sealink British Ferries announced more reductions in their operation on the Irish Sea in a revised agreement with B&I Line. The major change as far as the St. George's Channel services were concerned was the closure of the Rosslare–Pembroke Dock route with the loss of 535 jobs. Sealink British Ferries in return agreed to introduce "a new jumbo ferry" which was rumoured at the time to be T.T. Line's *Peter Pan*. In the event nothing came of these plans.

The pattern of sailings as far as Holyhead were concerned were to see the *St. Columba* and B&I sisters, *Leinster* and *Connacht*, operating alternately with the Danish-built ship between Dun Laoghaire and Dublin.

Sealink had planned to tie in their refits at both Fishguard and Holyhead with their operating partners B&I during the early months of 1986. The Irish Company were faced with a further period of industrial disputes and Sealink were forced to revise their plans. Sealink planned to withdraw the *St. Columba* for a five week period whilst she underwent an £80,000 internal refit in the early New Year. Her place was planned to be taken by the *Leinster* under the joint agreement between Sealink and B&I. However, the crew of the *Leinster* went on strike, which delayed the departure of the 'Columba'. There was no sign of the industrial dispute being concluded so the 'Columba' was withdrawn for a short overhaul only until 14th April when the *St. David* was able to relieve her for her major refit in Germany. On

Holyhead–Dun Laoghaire – From Car Ferry to HSS

20th May the *St. Columba* returned to her home port following her internal improvements, which included a Pullman Lounge and new restaurant. The *St. David* then sailed north to operate on the Stranraer-Larne service.

Under the terms of the joint arrangement, B&I and the Irish Government approved similar internal improvements to the *Leinster* and *Connacht* to bring them up to the standard of the Sealink British Ferries operation. Meanwhile, on the Irish Sea, Sealink and B&I agreed that their joint operation should be marketed as Southern Seaways.

The *St. David* once again relieved the *St. Columba* during her overhaul period from 27th February to 12th March 1987. Meanwhile, the chartered *Stena Sailer* started supplementary sailings on the Holyhead-Dun Laoghaire service to support the *St. Columba*. B&I tried to obtain a High Court injunction halting the new specialist freight service during April.

During the early autumn B&I Line were facing further major financial problems and the company was forced to look for rationalisations in their services together with staff cuts. It was also becoming more evident that the company would have to concentrate their efforts on the shorter Dublin–Holyhead service rather than the Liverpool route which was becoming less popular and more expensive to operate. At the end of 1987 B&I withdrew from the pooling agreement with Sealink. Meanwhile the Folkestone vessel, *Vortigern* ended her career with Sealink at Holyhead when she was called in to assist with freight on the Dun Laoghaire route during March 1988. After her final sailing on the last day of the month, she sailed the following day to Greece as the *Milos Express*.

At the beginning of August, the large ro-ro vessel *Seafreight Highway* appeared on the Holyhead–Dun Laoghaire run from

These two views show the **St. Columba** following her major refit in 1986. The above shows the new Pullman lounge and below the new Carte Blanche Restaurant. *(Ferry Publications Library)*

Holyhead–Dun Laoghaire – From Car Ferry to HSS

Dover to support the *St. Columba*, which in turn allowed the *Stena Sailer* to be moved to the Fishguard-Rosslare route.

Following the entry into service of the *Seafreight Highway*, plans then were drawn up for the French registered train ferry *Saint Eloi* to replace her on the route; in the event the *Stena Sailer* replaced the large freight vessel which had proved totally unsuitable. The *Stena Sailer* was later purchased by Sealink and renamed *St Cybi*. Meanwhile, the `Highway' was sent to the River Fal to lay up with her sister vessel the *Seafreight Freeway* which had earlier closed the Dover–Zeebrugge freight service on 16th September.

NEW LIVERPOOL SERVICE

In the early New Year the Irish Government approved a restructuring plan for B&I Line agreeing to the closure of the Dublin–Liverpool service and to allow B&I to concentrate their sailings on the Central Corridor to Holyhead. Following this announcement, Sealink confirmed that they were considering establishing their own service from Liverpool to Dun Laoghaire in place of the B&I link. The company entered manning level discussions with the N.U.S. during early January to use the *Earl William* on the route, which was now no longer required on the Channel Islands. The feasibility study continued by the company despite B&I still claiming that they might possibly run a summer Dublin–Liverpool service. The *Earl William*, which commenced service on 25th April, was ideally appointed for the new link with her well appointed cabins. Passenger numbers were limited to 600, which allowed most to acquire a berth for the overnight sailing. The service was slow to pick up but by the early summer bookings were showing encouraging signs.

Above: The chartered **Stena Sailer** seen at the layby berth at Holyhead. *(Dick Richards)*

Below: The controversial **Saint Eloi** pictured at the refit berth in April 1989. *(Dick Richards)*

Holyhead–Dun Laoghaire – From Car Ferry to HSS

Sadly, the route was suspended from 11th August after the *Earl William* developed problems with both her variable pitch propellers, one seizing completely and the other requiring attention. The 'William' was sent to Cardiff for dry docking, where initially it was thought the repairs would only take a week. She reopened the service on 24th August.

It was becoming evident by the early autumn that the Liverpool-Dun Laoghaire route was not attracting the anticipated business. The engine problems at the height of the summer were to cause major losses for the company and there was reluctance by staff at Holyhead to support the service from Liverpool. Despite the early losses, it was decided that the route would continue. The *Earl Granville* was sent to Liverpool in November to cover for the absence of the *Earl William* whilst on refit but the former Channel Islands vessel was to prove totally unsuitable as she could not maintain the schedules on the service, especially during bad weather.

During early March 1989, Stena Line AB of Gothenburg, Sweden, purchased 8% of Sea Containers' shares and Stena's Chief Executive announced that if proposed talks with James Sherwood failed then he would call on finances to launch an outright take-over of Sea Containers. The initial 8% was intended to be a "warning flag" of his intentions. Sherwood hoped that by gaining a Scandinavian ally, he could fight for a larger share of the market but in an increasingly competitive Scandinavia, Stena were now looking to extend their sphere of operations southwards. The year 1989 was marked by growing unrest and a rearguard action by Sea Containers to save itself from the advances of Tiphook (who sought their container business) and Stena who wished to absorb the Sealink ferry trade.

Following her service at Stranraer, the French vessel *Saint Eloi*

Above: The **Mona's Queen** strike-bound at Holyhead on 5th May 1988 whilst on charter to Sealink. *(Dick Richards)*
Below: The **Earl William** and **St. Columba** at Dun Laoghaire. *(Ferry Publications Library)*

Holyhead–Dun Laoghaire – From Car Ferry to HSS

then transferred to the Holyhead–Dun Laoghaire service in place of the *St. Columba* from 3rd-28th April. It was not a happy period of her career and resulted in many complaints from the travelling public.

Sealink closed the dedicated container service to Dublin as from 21st December. The two container vessels *Brian Boroime* and *Rhodri Mawr* were disposed of as part of the financial package against the Stena/Tiphook takeover bid. Both ships were eventually sold to the Greek Sarlis Group and left as the *Peltainer* and *Peliner*. Following this announcement, Sealink confirmed that for the 1990 season they would introduce additional passenger sailings between Holyhead and Dun Laoghaire using the *Horsa* from Folkestone.

During April 1990 the hostile takeover battle for the control of Sea Containers was finally resolved. Most of the company's container business went to Tiphook for £321 million while Sealink British Ferries was acquired by Stena Line of Sweden for £259 million. As part of the deal Sea Containers retained the ports of Heysham, Newhaven and Folkestone plus the land development at Harwich. The lucrative Isle of Wight services, Hoverspeed and their holding in the Isle of Man Steam Packet Company were also retained by Sea Containers.

Stena Line immediately began a thorough re-evaluation of all ships and routes. The most outward sign of change was the adoption of the trading name Sealink Stena Line while the ships of the fleet eventually gained the 'Stena' prefix.

On the last day of January, a serious engine room fire broke out in the *St. Columba*. The vessel departed from Dun Laoghaire at 08.45 to Anglesey but about ten miles out was forced to drop anchor after fire was found in the port engine. Captain Bakewell issued a general May Day and fire fighting teams were sent by

Above: The **Lady of Mann** seen here leaving Dun Laoghaire for Holyhead in March 1990 whilst on charter to Sealink. *(Gordon Hislip)*
Below: The former Folkestone-based **Horsa** swings off the Carlisle Pier for Holyhead. *(Miles Cowsill)*

An evening study of the **Stena Hibernia** arriving at Dun Laoghaire in July 1992. *(Gordon Hislip)*

Holyhead–Dun Laoghaire – From Car Ferry to HSS

helicopter to assist. The fire was eventually put out in force 8 conditions and with the wind strengthening, two tugs were called to assist the vessel into Holyhead and she finally arrived in her home port at 21.00. The *St. Columba* was sent to Liverpool for repairs following the incident and the *Darnia* was sent from Stranraer to reopen passenger sailings before the Isle of Man Steam Packet Company's *Lady of Mann* was chartered in her place. The Folkestone vessel *Horsa* arrived at Holyhead on 5th March to replace the *Lady of Mann* and some two weeks later the *St. Columba* arrived back following repairs.

On 23rd May the *Horsa* took up her planned summer schedule on the Holyhead–Dun Laoghaire service until 4th September.

On 5th September the *St. Columba* was involved in a further unfortunate incident when she suffered main bearing failure to one of her engines. She was to remain out of service for over a month, her place being taken by the smaller *Horsa*.

NEW THINKING BY STENA

Meanwhile at Holyhead, Stena Line unveiled an investment package for the Anglesey port. The new owners announced that the *St. Columba* would undergo a major £6 million refit which would include a complete rebuilding programme of all her passenger accommodation for the following season. The twelve year old ship would also be renamed *Stena Hibernia* following these works. To increase freight capacity on the link, the *St. Anselm*, renamed the *Stena Cambria* would be transferred from Folkestone to Holyhead to offer two additional round sailings a day. With a major investment by Sealink Stena Line in both Fishguard and Holyhead, B&I soon became very much a

Above: On 11th October 1989 Sealink announced the closure of the Liverpool-Dun Laoghaire service. The **Earl William** is seen here arriving at Liverpool for the final time on 9th January 1990. *(Ferry Publications Library)*

Below: The **Cambridge Ferry** was employed regularly on the Irish Sea in the early nineties. *(Gordon Hislip)*

36

Holyhead–Dun Laoghaire – From Car Ferry to HSS

This view shows the **St. Cybi** at the Salt Island berth with the **Stena Hibernia** arriving from Dun Laoghaire. *(Dick Richards)*

secondary operator on the Irish Sea, especially at Holyhead. The Government-owned company's hands were tied, having very little money to expand and improve their services. Meanwhile, B&I was put up for sale by the Irish Government and was later sold to Irish Ferries.

Further bad news hit the Irish Sea when it was announced that the Liverpool-Dun Laoghaire service would close as from 9th January 1991 with a loss of 100 jobs. The *Earl William* completed her last sailing between Ireland and Britain as scheduled and was then sent to Milford Haven for lay-up with the *Cambridge Ferry*.

The former Channel Islands' vessel however was back in service again on 28th January when she was chartered by Belfast Car Ferries following their vessel having to be withdrawn from service. She remained in service until March and once again was sent to Pembrokeshire for lay-up.

Following a disastrous first year's trading, during which time Stena made a pre-tax loss of £28.2 million, Sealink Stena Line's Managing Director Gareth Cooper wrote to his employees, "I must express to you the seriousness of the company's position." It was accepted within the industry that Stena's desire to acquire

Holyhead–Dun Laoghaire – From Car Ferry to HSS

the ferry operations of Sea Containers had resulted in an offer in excess of the company's market value and that severe retrenchments were now necessary. It was believed that Sealink was worth in the region of £180 million and yet Stena had paid £259 million, had immediately invested a further £178 million in new ships, opened a new route between Southampton and Cherbourg and taken on £200 million of Sealink's existing debt.

The company received a £60 million cash injection from Sweden and immediately launched its Operation Benchmark which looked for restructuring and economies. It was therefore decided during September to shed 1,000 staff at all levels and to close the Folkestone–Boulogne service at the end of the year.

Following the announcement that the *St. Columba* would undergo a major £6 million refit, the contract was secured by a German yard. The eight week refit saw all the existing facilities being replaced. A new a la carte restaurant, free-flow restaurant, children's playroom and nursery area, lorry drivers' restaurant, two new shops, Pullman lounge and businessmen's club, show bar, pizza parlour, gambling arcade and Irish bar were installed during this overhaul. The new show bar would provide a new travel concept created by Stena Line in Sweden, giving live entertainment on most sailings with rock bands, country & western and jazz music being offered. The refitted vessel would be the first in the Sealink fleet to convey the much-vaunted Stena Line 'travel service concept', which was designed to give people the chance of not just travelling from A to B, but the sheer pleasure of being onboard a ship.

Meanwhile, following the departure of the *St. Columba* for her major refit, the *Stena Cambria* replaced her on the route. On 11th February 1991, she holed herself in the inner harbour at Holyhead and as a result had to be sent to Birkenhead for repairs. The *Stena*

Above: The **Stena Hengist** seen leaving Dun Laoghaire for Holyhead on 26th January 1992. *(Gordon Hislip)*
Below: The **St. Cybi** seen departing from Dun Laoghaire on her late evening freight run to Wales. *(Gordon Hislip)*

Holyhead–Dun Laoghaire – From Car Ferry to HSS

Horsa was sent from Folkestone to cover her absence taking up the service the next day until the *Earl William* was able to enter service two days later from her lay up on the River Fal. The *Earl William,* with a limited passenger certificate for only 300, was later joined by the *Cambridge Ferry*. On 19th February the 'Cambria' returned to the link on completion of her repairs, which allowed the *Cambridge Ferry* to sail back to Stranraer and the 'William' to lay up once again.

On Thursday, 14th March the *Stena Hibernia* re-entered service following her extensive refit. On 29th June, the *Earl William* re-entered service on the Holyhead–Dun Laoghaire route with the *Stena Hibernia* as the *Stena Cambria* was retained at Dover until the arrival of the *Stena Invicta*. She took up service on the 12.45 sailing from Dun Laoghaire to Holyhead operating with a reduced passenger certificate until the arrival of the 'Cambria'. The 'Cambria' arrived back on 8th July, and took up service some three days later on the 04.00 sailing to Ireland. The *Earl William* then stood down. The continued freight boom at Holyhead saw Sealink having to charter the freight vessel *Auersbeg* to support the two passenger ferries on the link for the summer period.

Following the closure of the Folkestone-Boulogne service on 31st December 1991, the *Stena Hengist* was sent to Holyhead to cover for the overhauls of the *Stena Hibernia* and *Stena Cambria*. The former Folkestone ship then sailed north to Stranraer to cover for their refits, before returning to Holyhead for disposal. On 17th March, she sailed to Greece as the *Romilda*.

With the closure of the Folkestone–Boulogne service, the *Stena Horsa* arrived at Milford Haven on 5th January 1992 to lay up with the *Earl William* and *St. Cybi*, which had completed her last spell in service just before Christmas on the Holyhead-Dun Laoghaire route. The 'Horsa' was subsequently sold to

Above: The **Stena Galloway** seen arriving at Holyhead during her brief spell on the route in July 1992. *(Nick Robins)*
Below: The French registered **Chartres** seen leaving Dun Laoghaire for Holyhead in October 1992. *(Gordon Hislip)*

Holyhead–Dun Laoghaire – From Car Ferry to HSS

Agoudimos Lines for which she was renamed *Penelope A*. The *Earl William* was also sold to Greek interests later in the summer and renamed *Pearl William*. Meanwhile, the veteran train ferry *Cambridge Ferry* completed her last sailing on 16th March on the Stranraer–Larne service, the next day she sailed to Milford Haven, via Fishguard, for lay up. A month later, on 21st April, she sailed as the *Ita Uno* prior to taking up service between Bari (Italy) and Durres in Albania. She has since been renamed *Sirio*.

On 28th July 1992 the *Stena Cambria* commenced operations using the new deep water berth at Holyhead because of the tidal restrictions in the inner harbour. The same day the vessel experienced major engine problems and had to be withdrawn from service and the *Stena Galloway* from Stranraer was sent to replace her. After minor repairs to the 'Cambria', she was then sent to Stranraer in place of the 'Galloway' until mid-August when she returned to Birkenhead for major repairs before returning to her home port on 21st August.

Sea Containers, who had started the new SeaCat Scotland operation between Stranraer and Belfast, expressed interest in starting another rival service on the Irish Sea between Holyhead and Dun Laoghaire. Following Sealink refusing slots at both ports, the matter then went to the E.E.C. Commissioners and Sealink were forced to offer their rivals operational slots at Holyhead but in the event the service failed to materialise.

The French registered *Chartres* was chartered in October to cover for the *Stena Cambria* whilst she was at Fishguard. She was employed as freight only vessel whilst at Holyhead.

In late May 1993, Stena Sealink announced that they planned to open a new fast ferry service between Holyhead and Dun Laoghaire with the new 240 ft. wavepiercer catamaran *Stena Sea Lynx*. The new service would take passengers 1 hour 50 minutes

Above: The **Norrona** was chartered by Sealink for two seasons for overhauls on their Irish Sea services. The vessel is seen here arriving at Dun Laoghaire in February 1994. *(Gordon Hislip)*
Below: The **Stena Cambria** seen arriving at Dun Laoghaire in July 1995. *(Miles Cowsill)*

The *Stena Sea Lynx II* seen leaving Holyhead for Dun Laoghaire. *(Miles Cowsill)*

Holyhead–Dun Laoghaire – From Car Ferry to HSS

The **Stena Sea Lynx** seen arriving at Dun Laoghaire in her first season on the new high-speed service between Wales and Ireland. *(Gordon Hislip)*

to make the crossing between Wales and Ireland, instead of the conventional ferry timing of 3 hours 30 minutes. Initially it would operate four round sailings a day, which would be reduced for the winter period to three. The new craft would have capacity for 450 passengers and up to 90 cars. On 15th July, Mrs. Glenys Kinnock, wife of Neil Kinnock M.P., dedicated the new service. Some four weeks after the new fast craft entered service, she had carried some 58,328 passengers, 12,340 cars and 210 motorbikes, with 100% reliability record. Following the success of the fast ferry service, the company announced that a larger mark II craft would enter service the following summer with an increased capacity for 600 passengers and 140 cars.

Further important high-speed news was announced by Stena Sealink Line on 6th July at a press conference in London. The company announced that they had placed an order for two massive high-speed ferries from Finnyards, Rauma, Finland for delivery in 1995. One of the revolutionary craft would be placed on the Holyhead-Dun Laoghaire service within two years. At the press conference Stena Line A.B., who had ordered the new vessels, claimed they would be a technological breakthrough with both cars and freight being able to be carried on the 40 knot craft. The new HSS (high speed sea service) would boast a length of some 124 metres and a beam of 40 metres and would be able to carry 1,500 passengers and 375 cars or 50 trucks and 100 cars. The craft would be powered by water jets via four gas turbines, which would be able to operate in most weather conditions. Loading and unloading would be via a special stern ramp and anticipated turnrounds would be some 30 minutes at each port. Over the next three years the first craft

Holyhead–Dun Laoghaire – From Car Ferry to HSS

The **Stena Sea Lynx** and the **Stena Cambria** pictured at the St. Michael's Pier in October 1993. *(Gordon Hislip)*

was developed in great secrecy and eventually made her debut to the press on 20th February 1996.

Work started in 1994 in anticipation of the arrival of the new HSS. Similar work commenced at St. Michael's Pier at Dun Laoghaire to accommodate the new operation.

The company's rivals at Holyhead, B&I Line and their now parent company Irish Ferries, announced that they would build a new vessel for their route to Dublin, which would triple their freight capacity and provide an 81% increase in car capacity on the Central Corridor service. The new four engined vessel built in Holland would have an operating speed of 21.5 knots with a car capacity for 600 and accommodation for 1,700 passengers. With the forthcoming introduction of the HSS, B&I Line had no alternative but to order new tonnage. Later the B&I trade name was dropped in favour of Irish Ferries.

The *Stena Sea Lynx II* arrived at Holyhead from Tasmania on the morning of 18th June and was officially named two days later by the wife of the Anglesey M.P. The fast craft entered service

During 1996 the **Stena Hibernia** was renamed **Stena Adventurer** for her last season in service on the Irish Sea. She is seen here arriving at Holyhead in July 1996. *(Miles Cowsill)*

The **Stena Traveller** at Holyhead in July 1996. *(Miles Cowsill)*

Holyhead–Dun Laoghaire – From Car Ferry to HSS

on 22nd June on the 07.00 sailing from Holyhead which allowed the renamed *Stena Sea Lynx* to sail south to take up service between Fishguard and Rosslare. Meanwhile at Holyhead, the company were to see a 12% increase in passenger figures.

A new Holyhead-Dublin freight ferry service started as from 2nd November 1995 using the *Stena Traveller*. The introduction of this new dedicated freight operation was in response to Irish Ferries' success with their new passenger/freight vessel *Isle of Innisfree*. Two round sailings a day would be operated by the *Stena Traveller*, a sister of the *Stena Challenger* at Dover. The route initially commenced using the chartered freighter *Marine Evangeline* on 13th October 1995.

The *Stena Hibernia*, which had played an important role at Holyhead for over eighteen years, was repainted and renamed *Stena Adventurer* in anticipation of her transfer to Dover from the Irish Sea on the arrival of the HSS. In the event, the vessel was not put on the Dover Strait but was to remain at Holyhead in a supportive role to the HSS.

The *Stena Traveller* had to be taken out of service during February when she unfortunately grounded whilst berthing at the Anglesey port. During October, the 'Traveller' was replaced by her near sister from Dover the *Stena Challenger*. The 'Challenger' entered operations as a freight ship and further back-up if required to the HSS service.

After a blaze of publicity, both in the national press and television, in the Dover Strait, the *Stena Explorer* then sailed to Holyhead for a further fitting-out and extensive safety tests with the DOT and the Irish Marine. The *Stena Londoner*, after covering for the refit of the *Stena Felicity*, left Fishguard on 3rd April for Holyhead to operate with the *Stena Adventurer* and *Stena Lynx* on the Holyhead-Dun Laoghaire service.

Above: The freighter **Marine Evangeline** seen departing from Holyhead on 15th October 1995, prior to the arrival of the **Stena Traveller**. *(Gordon Hislip)*
Below: A night view of the **Stena Londoner** at Dun Laoghaire in March 1996. *(Gordon Hislip)*

Holyhead–Dun Laoghaire – From Car Ferry to HSS

ENTER THE EXPLORER

The *Stena Explorer* entered service on 10th April on a low-key basis following an imposition of a 2.6 metre wave height operating restriction by the Department of Transport, pending a bad weather testing of the marine evaluation system of new craft. In the event, rather than take her out of service, the equipment was eventually fitted to the Stranraer-based ferry *Stena Galloway* for final evacuation and approval by both British and Irish authorities.

The *Stena Explorer* carried 36,000 passengers and some 6,000 vehicles during its first full week in service. The craft achieved a speed of 47.8 knots in April, with the fastest recorded crossing between Wales and Ireland at 94 minutes on 23rd April.

Like her forthcoming sisters for Belfast and Harwich services, she has only one passenger deck with a total area of approximately 4,000 square metres. The walkways and seating areas lie along the sides of the passenger deck, beside the panoramic windows which are 2.5 metres high and over 30 metres long. Further in, towards the centre of the craft, the deck rises in several stages so views are equally good wherever you may be on the passenger deck. At the top of the rear stairs from the car-deck is the information area. The aft section of the passenger deck is also the location for the duty free shopping mall and children's activity and entertainment centre.

The middle section of the craft is dominated by two fast food restaurants, including a MacDonalds. There is also a bar, a playroom for younger children, and a massive video wall made of 27 interconnected video monitors for displaying information and safety messages, sales announcements and advertising. Stena Line claim that this is the largest video wall of its kind to be found

Above: The **Stena Explorer** seen under construction in Finland. *(Stena Line)*
Below: This view shows two of the waterjets which drive the **Stena Explorer**. *(Stena Line)*

This aerial view of Holyhead shows the **Stena Explorer** getting underway for Dun Laoghaire. *(Stena Line)*

Holyhead–Dun Laoghaire – From Car Ferry to HSS

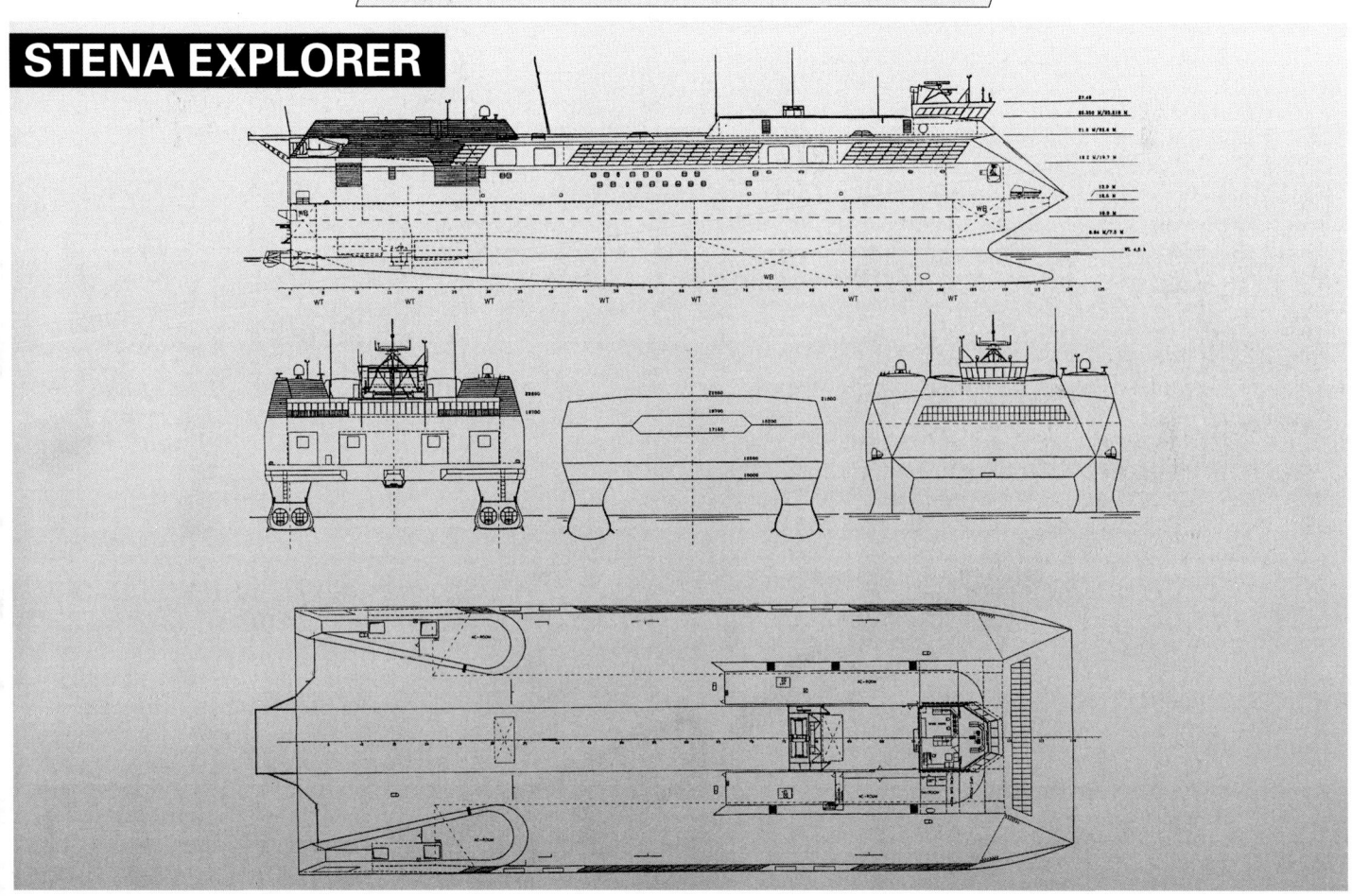

STENA EXPLORER

on a ship anywhere in the world.

Further forward there is the Globetrotter Restaurant, business lounge and a service centre for truck drivers, including their own restaurant and shower areas. In the front section of the vessel, there are two more bars, one on either side of the vessel, including the motorists lounge/bar. Possibly for most people, by far the greatest experience on board are the passenger areas forward in the bow and stern. The forward section is dominated by a large panoramic window, where passengers can lean on a rail in front and enjoy sea views heading towards them at some 40 knots. At the stern exhilarating views are offered as the craft's water jets throw up the water.

The engines of the HSS 1500 are designed directly from the advanced jet engine. Placing the jet age gas turbines in the double hull generates high speeds and high levels of safety with fewer operational disruptions than other fast craft, Stena Line claim. The low weight of the engines also means a corresponding increase in the vessel's loading capacity . The gas turbines from General Electric, have been re-built for maritime use on the HSS . Each of the vessel's two hulls contain two gas turbines, one large and one small. Stena Line in its development of the HSS, chose to use water jets instead of the conventional propeller as the water jet units would be more efficient at high speeds and also they would offer improved manoeuvrability. The four water jets that drive the Stena HSS, two in each aft section of the vessel, draft in water through inlets in the ferry's hull. The actual inlets have a diameter of 1.6 metres. The impeller (the propeller in a water jet) is located inside the unit in a space large enough for a fully grown man to stand upright. Right at the back of the five metre long water jet units, lie the massive steering and reversing drives. Each steering drive can be turned 30 degrees to starboard or port, and thus

Above: The duty-free shop on the **Stena Explorer**. *(Mike Louagie)*
Below: The upper seating area of the cafeteria on the **Stena Explorer**. *(Mike Louagie)*

Holyhead–Dun Laoghaire – From Car Ferry to HSS

steer the ferry in the desired direction.

The *Stena Explorer* loads and unloads in record time for her capacity, the minimum time in port, the company claim, can be as little as 20 minutes, however they have made provision in their timetables for a maximum turnaround of 30 minutes. Every minute of delay is expensive for the company. If, for example, the craft turnaround time was to be delayed by 10 minutes she would have to increase her speed by 5 knots to keep up with the sailing frequency. This completely new docking technique has been developed by the Company. The new linkspan is designed specifically for the HSS and also includes a quick coupling with fuel, fresh water and waste water pipes.

When the HSS docks, she reverses towards the linkspan construction. The reversing manoeuvre is made easier by the fact that the ferry is fitted with navigational equipment (which can determine the position of the ferry to within one metre via 4 TV cameras and a special docking radar mounted in the stern). Once the craft has made contact with the linkspan fenders the quick couplings are connected on either side of the ferry's stern, pulling it automatically into the correct position so the gangway (drive on ramps) is quickly fitted. In stark contrast to most linkspans, this is controlled by the craft, not a land based operation.

Supplies for the on-board restaurant and duty-free are loaded into containers. A "transverse" rail on the outer roof of the craft lowers them directly into a position inside the craft. The restaurant container is lowered through an outlet in the bow roof, while the container with the duty-free articles is loaded at the stern. Both of these containers stay on board until stocks need replenishing once more. Passengers go on board and ashore along two parallel passage gangways located on either side of the linkspan. Passengers drive on board and ashore via four stern

Above: The **Stena Explorer** at the Dun Laoghaire berth in July 1996. *(Gordon Hislip)*

Below: The **Stena Challenger** seen leaving Dublin in her first few days in service on the link in September 1996. *(Gordon Hislip)*

Holyhead–Dun Laoghaire – From Car Ferry to HSS

doors. Three of the doors are used simultaneously during loading. Two of them lead into the ferry's main loading deck, whilst the third feeds cars up to an extra mezzanine deck situated above the main deck.

By July the *Stena Explorer* had carried over half million passengers with very few cancellations during the summer period. Meanwhile, the *Stena Adventurer* was withdrawn from service on 30th September and was put on the disposal list. She later sailed for lay-up at Belfast.

The *Stena Challenger* was transferred from Dover and entered service on the Holyhead - Dublin freight service on 17th September with a passenger certificate for 500 passengers. The former Dover vessel had a new stern ramp fitted to her while refitting at Falmouth for her new role. The *Stena Traveller* was then returned to Sweden by Stena Line U.K.

The **Stena Adventurer** and **Stena Explorer** seen together at Dun Laoghaire in June 1996. *(Gordon Hislip)*

Holyhead–Dun Laoghaire – From Car Ferry to HSS

FERRY Publications Ltd

We have a wide selection of titles on ferries covering all aspects of the industry in Britain and Europe. For our current booklist of over forty titles telephone or write to us today.

To keep in touch with the ferry world you need

EUROPEAN FERRY SCENE

Our quarterly magazine is packed with facts, photographs and details of everything that's going on in the ferry world. The 56 pages are eagerly awaited by both enthusiasts and those who work in the industry. For further details on how to subscribe, telephone or write to us.

Ferry Publications Ltd, PO Box 9, Narberth, SA68 0YT.

ACKNOWLEDGMENTS:

The authors would like to thank the following for their help with this publication:
Dick Richards; Gordon Hislip; Philip Booth; Jim Ashby; Malcolm McRonald; Phil Neumann, FotoFlite; Nick Robins; Mike Louagie; and Pat Somner, Ferry Publications. Finally, the authors would like to thank the staff of Haven Colourprint for their assistance with the production of this title.

All rights reserved. No part of this publication may be produced without prior permission in writing from Ferry Publications Ltd.

The **Duke of Lancaster** at the Carlisle Pier in July 1978. *(John Hendy)*

Holyhead–Dun Laoghaire – From Car Ferry to HSS

Cranes would swing the mail and baggage into the yawning holds, capstans would turn, whistles would send their shrieking messages through the night air, lines would be 'let go' and slowly the steamer would back off into the outer harbour ready to swing and face the sea.

The inner harbour in those days would have been full of other ships. The Greenore steamer, the Dublin (North Wall) cattle boats, ships in reserve and ships on overhaul would have made an avenue through which the Kingstown-bound vessel would have passed. The nightly rituals of departure having passed, those on board would settle down for the crossing. Indeed, many would already be fast asleep below, totally impervious to all that had gone on about their recumbent forms.

The original car ferry berth being placed at Salt Island, the comings and goings of the seasonal car ferry service in no way affected the year by year passenger and mail link. But the withdrawal of the *Cambria* and then the *Hibernia* and the entry into service of the new *St. Columba* meant that a new linkspan was constructed at the former departure berth by the now deserted station hotel. With a passenger certificate for as many as 2,400 and space on her vehicle decks for 310 cars, the new ship fulfilled a dual purpose and effectively did away with three vessels.

In 1978, passengers alighting at Holyhead from the London boat train carried their own luggage and were directed away from the ship across the old station forecourt, past its handless clock before being funnelled into an asbestos sheeted tunnel which mysteriously led them back in the direction from which they had come.

The *St. Columba* was a 'brown' ship. The colour was everywhere and created an impression of warmth and restfulness. There was little time to explore her before departure and on the stroke of 15.15 hours, the ferry moved off its berth and began her own daily crossing, gently throbbing past the Belfast-bound container ship *Brian Boroime*, a deserted Salt Island, the empty dry dock and headed into a calm and clear sea.

A visit was made to the Cardiff Arms Bar in which one sank into an orange vinyl seat and sipped a strong brew from a plastic beaker. Ventilation was excellent, the bar was brightly lit and the carpets gently crept up the table legs.

A quick tour of the Second Class showed long queues snaking their way around the accommodation - every outlet was busy and the oncoming tides of passengers quietly joined the patient lines.

With the ship driving on at almost 19 knots, we crossed the *Duke of Lancaster*, then in the twilight of her career and the sole survivor of the post-war Heysham trio. The *St. Columba* had something of a reputation as a poor time-keeper in those early days of her career but this was almost entirely due to the inability to load and discharge ro-ro freight in the limited turn-round times. She was then the largest ferry in the Irish Sea and this accolade proved to be something of her Achilles heel for when she broke down (a fairly regular occurrence in those days), it needed two ships to replace her.

It seemed that in no time at all, the Wicklow Mountains were peering above the western horizon with the Head of Howth soon becoming visible to their north. Between these uplands lay Dublin Bay with the vast chimneys of the power station a landmark from way out.

A visit to the bridge produced a warm welcome from Captain John Peters and a kind invitation to remain there to watch the ship berth. By now we were nearing the Kish Light and then came the South Burfold Buoy at the entrance to Dublin Bay. All too soon we were sailing in past Dun Laoghaire's East Pier and through the narrow harbour entrance gradually nosing towards the Carlisle Pier on which the black and orange Dublin-bound train patiently sat. It is always a tense moment with the ship hemmed in on three sides and with very little forward way: a sudden gust of wind could catch her massive freeboard and dash her against the pier in front of the expectant crowd of onlookers gathered at the pier gates. But there were no dramas today - Captain Peters brought her in without so much of a bump.

Holyhead–Dun Laoghaire – From Car Ferry to HSS

HOLYHEAD-DUN LAOGHAIRE
First Impressions

The following is adapted from an article which first appeared in the October 1978 issue of 'Sea Breezes' magazine.

Desolation at Holyhead! The lovely old London & North Western Railway Hotel lies at the head of the inner harbour in a state of ruin - chimneyless, with windows smashed and ornate ironwork rusted and broken. It was a shame that British Rail had no further use for the 98 year old building but Victorian hotels had no place on busy vehicle-crammed quaysides. Gone were the passengers who would rather stay put for a day or two while gales in the Irish Sea raged and the steamers battled it out against wind and rain. With vessels the size of the *St. Columba* in service, you could be confident that she'd give you a fairly trouble-free crossing in all but the worst of winter storms.

In 1978, passenger arrangements at Holyhead were pretty primitive. The L.N.W.R. had it all worked out to a tee. The incoming mail boat would tie up at the arrivals berth from where passengers would join their trains. Before sailing again the following night, the steamer would be warped across to the departure berth alongside which the outward 'Irish Mail' would later hiss and pant before emptying its human cargo onto the platform. There the travellers would gaze up at the bulk of the smartly kept steamer, straining at its moorings in anticipation of its nightly sprint across the 57 miles between quaysides.

The rituals of travel in those far off days were quite different to those experienced today. Porters in their dozens would swarm around the First Class passengers and would be directed to assorted baggage and luggage waiting to be shipped. The Third Class would make their way via their own entrance into the spartan after end of the steamer's accommodation.

Above: The **Princess Maud** arriving off Holyhead in the late fifties. *(Malcolm McRonald collection)*

Below: The **Cambria** at the Carlisle Pier, Dun Laoghaire in July 1959. *(Malcolm McRonald collection)*

The **Stena Explorer** pictured at 43 knots in the Irish Sea. *(Miles Cowsill)*